Layla and the Blue Bird

by Cameron Macintosh

illustrated by Beth Hughes

OXFORD
UNIVERSITY PRESS
AUSTRALIA & NEW ZEALAND

Layla was sitting on a beanbag. She had found a book about birds to read.

Layla began to enjoy the book, but she soon started to yawn.

Just then, Layla spied a bright blue bird. It was flapping around in the playground.

Layla darted out to *see* the bird.

"Wow!" said Layla. "There are lots of birds in the playground!"

The birds lifted their wings and went up to the clouds. The blue bird went up, too.

"Let me come with you," cried Layla.

Just then, Layla saw a balloon in the playground. She got in and it floated up.

Layla was enjoying the flight when the balloon began to go down.

"Oh no," she said. "My balloon has a leak!"

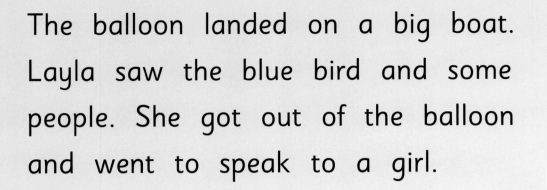

The balloon landed on a big boat.
Layla saw the blue bird and some
people. She got out of the balloon
and went to speak to a girl.

"Did you come to rescue me?" said Layla.

"Yes, we did," said the girl. "The blue bird said you needed help. Come and sit down."

Layla sat down on a soft chair.

She soon fell asleep.

"Up you get, Layla," said Mrs Floyd.

"What a day," said Layla. "I just went to the clouds in a balloon!"

"I think you were dreaming," said Mrs Floyd.

"You might be right," said Layla, with a grin.